מסורה

ArtScroll Youth Series®

A Dov Dov Book

DOV DOV AND THE MONEY TREE
and other stories

by Yona Weinberg

illustrated by Liat Benyaminy Ariel

FIRST EDITION
First Impression . . . September, 1990

Published and Distributed by
MESORAH PUBLICATIONS, Ltd.
Brooklyn, New York 11232

Distributed in Israel by
MESORAH MAFITZIM / J. GROSSMAN
Rechov Harav Uziel 117
Jerusalem, Israel

Distributed in Europe by
J. LEHMANN HEBREW BOOKSELLERS
20 Cambridge Terrace
Gateshead, Tyne and Wear
England NE8 1RP

Distributed in Australia & New Zealand by
GOLD'S BOOK & GIFT CO.
36 William Street
Balaclava 3183, Vic., Australia

Distributed in South Africa by
KOLLEL BOOKSHOP
22 Muller Street
Yeoville 2198
Johannesburg, South Africa

ARTSCROLL YOUTH SERIES®
DOV DOV AND THE MONEY TREE AND OTHER STORIES
© Copyright 1990, by YONA WEINBERG and MESORAH PUBLICATIONS, Ltd.
4401 Second Avenue / Brooklyn, N.Y. 11232 / (718) 921-9000

ALL RIGHTS RESERVED.

*No part of this book may be reproduced
in any form* — including photocopying and retrieval systems —
without **written** *permission from the copyright holder,
except by a reviewer who wishes to quote brief passages in connection with a review
written for inclusion in magazines or newspapers.*

THE RIGHTS OF THE COPYRIGHT HOLDER WILL BE STRICTLY ENFORCED.

ISBN:
0-89906-972-X (hard cover)
0-89906-973-8 (paperback)

Typography by CompuScribe at ArtScroll Studios, Ltd.
4401 Second Avenue / Brooklyn, N.Y. 11232 / (718) 921-9000

Printed in the United States of America by
EDISON LITHOGRAPHING AND PRINTING CORP.
Bound by Sefercraft, Quality Bookbinders, Ltd. Brooklyn, N.Y.

Table of Contents

Dov Dov and the Money Tree 7

Pajamas on Highway Ninety-Five 17

Good-bye, Mrs. Kay 25

Partners Forever 34

Tornado Alert 47

Watch out Below 53

Dov Dov and the Snowbird 60

Dov Dov and the Money Tree

Dov Dov had a problem. It wasn't a very unusual problem. In fact, it was a problem lots of people had. He frowned and bit his lip. It was a problem he had had for a long time.

He needed money. Lots of money. There were so many things he wanted to buy and have but everything costs money — and most of the things he wanted were not cheap.

"Why couldn't everything be free?" he asked Tully, his friend.

"I guess if everything were free we wouldn't want things so much," said Tully, a sandy-haired boy.

"That doesn't make sense," said Dov Dov, a good-natured boy with a lively imagination that matched his sparkling brown eyes. "Why wouldn't we want them? I'd buy everything if it were free."

"Why would you buy it if it were yours for free?" asked Tully.

"Oh, you know what I mean!" Dov Dov persisted.

They were looking into the window of a watch store. In the window was a black digital watch Dov Dov had his eyes on. It looked similar to the watch he was wearing, but the watch in the window had a calculator in addition to an alarm stop watch.

"How I wish I could have a million dollars," Dov Dov said.

The two boys walked along the hot pavement, each with his own thoughts. When they reached Dov Dov's house, Dov Dov said, "Hey, Tully, do you want to sleep over tonight? We could play ball and have fun."

"O.K. I'll call my mom and ask her if it's O.K."

Dov Dov and Tully spent a long evening playing and reading. The summer air was hot.

"Hey!" Dov Dov had an idea. "Maybe my parents will let us sleep in the backyard tonight. I heard that some of the other boys did it last week when it was 98 degrees."

"What about the mosquitoes?" asked Tully, the practical one.

"What about them?" asked Dov Dov.

"I mean, we'll get bitten up."

"Well, yeah, sure, but that's part of the fun."

Dov Dov's parents weren't too sure it was a good idea.

"What can happen, Mom? We're right by the house."

After some discussion and rules, his parents agreed on condition they slept close to the house and left the back door unlocked.

"In case of rain or anything," Dov Dov assured Tully.

The boys were excited. They took their sleeping bags and pillows out to the grass.

"Want a snack?"

"O.K.!"

"My mother baked my favorite chocolate-chip cookies."

He opened a bag full of cookies, enough to feed their whole class.

"Hmm, Yum!" said Tully. "Your mother is a great baker."

"Don't eat too much or you'll get a stomach ache," warned Dov Dov.

"And," added Tully, "we'll have crazy dreams."

But the boys didn't heed their own advice and munched and talked till the bag was finished and only a few crumbs and stray cookies were left on the ground.

Dov Dov picked a dandelion and blew through it. "I sure wish I had lots and lots of money. I wish money would just grow on a tree."

"Not me," said Tully, "too much money brings too much trouble."

He scratched a mosquito bite on his knee.

Dov Dov's eyes grew heavy. He finished his last cookie and threw the crumbs into the grass, by the broken gate.

"Let's go to sleep now."

The boys said *Shema* and dove into their sleeping bags. The moon sailed like a silver crescent in a dark sea. The stars shone like brilliant jewels. The last thing Dov Dov remembered was a faint roar and a rumbling in the distance. He closed his eyes and went to sleep.

"Dov Dov, wake up, wake up, quick."

"What — what — what?" said Dov Dov.

"Dov Dov, wake up!" the voice said. "You've got to see this. You're not going to believe it."

Tully was standing in front of him. His eyes were puffy with sleep but there was bright excitement in them.

Dov Dov sat up. "What is it, Tully? It's too early to get up. It's barely sunrise! Why are you waking me so early? Let's sleep late."

But Tully was already pulling Dov Dov up on his feet.

"Where are you taking me?" Dov Dov walked and tripped on a root.

"Ow! My ankle! Where did that root come from? Where did all these roots come from?"

He stopped short in his tracks. The air was fresh and clear like after rain. The dew glistened on the grass like a million diamonds. And there in front of him was the strangest scene he had ever seen in all his life.

A tall oak tree stood by the broken gate. It seemed like an ordinary tree but . . . it couldn't be — it just couldn't be real. This tree wasn't here last night. How could a tree grow in one night? It wasn't possible. What kind of tree was it anyway? What kind of leaves were these? Oh, he shouldn't have eaten the whole bag of cookies his mother had given him last night. He was seeing things . . . and what was Tully doing picking off a leaf and eating it?

Dov Dov and Tully exchanged puzzled looks. Tully began scrambling up through the branches.

"Tully, what are you doing?"

"Try it," said Tully, as he blew a leaf to him. "It tastes like . . . like a chocolate-chip cookie."

The leaf was wrapped in a green paper peel. Dov Dov threw away the peel and picked another leaf. He looked at the leaf closely. It looked like . . . a ten-dollar bill. His eyes and mouth grew round like flying saucers. The whole tree was covered with

ten, twenty, and one hundred-dollar bills, all green and crisp. When Dov Dov pulled another leaf a new one grew in its place.

"Is this for real, or am I dreaming?" he asked, scratching his head.

"If you're dreaming," said Tully, "don't wake up 'cause I'm in it too and I don't want to leave."

"Pinch me. Ouch! Yep, it's for real, but how in the world could a tree grow overnight in somebody's backyard, especially a money tree?"

"Don't ask questions," said Tully, "this is what you've always wanted. Let's start picking leaves right away. Let's not waste time."

"Whoopee!" yelled Dov Dov as he frantically started pulling leaves off the tree.

The two boys worked for an hour until they were exhausted.

"There's no sense in being greedy. We'll pick some later. Now let's go and buy some stuff."

The boys spent the morning shopping, going from one store to another. There was no end to the amount of goods they could buy.

"I can't believe our good luck. I could buy everything I've always wanted . . . and even more," said Tully.

"Why, I'll be the happiest kid in the world."

"Me too," echoed Tully.

The boys came home laden down with packages, exhausted but happy.

"We'd better use the basement door. I don't know how I'll ever be able to explain this to my mother."

Dov Dov's room was covered wall to wall with portable computer games, electronic games, puzzles, books, walkie-talkies and construction sets. The boys began playing, laughing and yelling, "I can't believe our good luck."

After a few hours, Tully lay back on Dov Dov's bed.

"I'm beat!" he said. "Let's go out and play ball."

"Ball!" Dov Dov couldn't believe his ears. "How can you think of playing ball when we've got all this stuff around?"

Tully took a pensive look at all the toys.

"I don't know," he said. "It just doesn't seem like so much fun after a while. In fact, I kinda enjoyed buying the stuff more that the actual playing. I'm getting a headache and my eyes are hurting me. Come on, let's go outside. Maybe we can gather up some of the neighborhood boys and start a game of baseball."

"We've got the best, most expensive equipment in town," said Dov Dov, "and all you can think of is ball."

"I'm sorry," said Tully. "At first it was all so exciting. But now, . . . I don't know. It's just too much. I'm just plain bored."

He gave Dov Dov a sad look and left the room.

"Well, he might get bored, but I'll never get bored!" thought Dov Dov and he started to play by himself. After a half an hour Dov Dov had to admit to himself that even he was getting bored.

"I don't get it! I just don't get it!" he muttered. "What's going wrong?"

His mother was in the kitchen unpacking groceries. Dov Dov went to help her put away the packages.

"Mom," he said carefully, "if you had all the money in the world, would you be happy?"

Dov Dov's mother laughed. "I'd settle for just three thousand right now to pay the grocer, the butcher and the dentist."

"No, really, Mom," Dov Dov persisted, "if you could buy anything you want, would you buy a bigger house, more furniture, a fancier car? You name it! Anything! What would you do?"

"Hmm, that's a tough question."

She sat down by the kitchen table.

"Suppose," continued Dov Dov, "I gave you right now one million dollars. What would you do with it?"

"Well," began Dov Dov's mother, "I certainly wouldn't buy more furniture or a fancy car."

"Why not?"

"Well, in the first place, I don't need more furniture. I don't need a fancy car."

"Why not?" demanded Dov Dov. "It's your money! You could do whatever you want with it."

"That's just it, Dov Dov. It's not my money."

"But I'm giving it to you," Dov Dov persisted.

"But it's not your money either," said Dov Dov's mother. "It belongs to *Hashem*. He only gave it to you as a gift to put to good use. Everything we have is a gift from *Hashem*. Whether it's money, talent, brains, anything. It's just a gift from *Hashem* to see if we use the gift wisely."

Dov Dov was quiet.

"So," continued his mother, "I think the first thing I would do is give a large percent of the money to poor people and to *yeshivos* to help boys become *talmidei chachamim*. Then I'd . . ."

But Dov Dov didn't hear the rest. His thoughts were racing.

"That's why Tully and I didn't really enjoy ourselves with all the stuff we bought. We thought first only of ourselves. The money was just given to us as a test, like everything else, to see how we use it, if we use it wisely, the way *Hashem* wants us to."

"Excuse me, Mom," Dov Dov interrupted his mother.

He walked out to the backyard. Yes, the tree was still there, standing tall and proud in the bright sunlight. Was it just this morning? It seemed a long time ago when he had first seen the tree.

Dov Dov walked over to it. The tree seemed different, stronger and taller; its branches stretching out like clutching arms. Dov Dov pulled off a leaf. Suddenly the tree began to sway back and forth, rumbling and pouring its sap on him. Whooo! Eeeee! Hoooo!

"Help!" Dov Dov screamed, "I'm being attacked by a tree! Help! Get away from me, you giant tree. Let go of me! Let go!"

"Dov Dov, Dov Dov," someone was shaking him.

"What . . . what . . . what . . . what . . . what," Dov Dov mumbled.

He opened his eyes and felt rain pouring down his neck.

Dov Dov and the Money Tree / 15

"You were dreaming," said Tully, "something about a tree attacking you. That must've been some weird dream. Come on! Let's get out of the rain."

"You mean there is no money tree!"

"Money tree! Wow! That must have been some crazy dream you had."

"It was right over there." Dov Dov pointed to a little hole in the corner near the broken gate.

"It's gone."

"What's gone?"

"Our money tree."

"I told you! It was just a dream," said Tully.

Dov Dov stood up, shaking the water off his clothing. He started picking up his soggy sleeping bag.

"Come on. Let's get in fast. This thunder is scaring me," said Tully.

"O.K., I'm coming. Just one minute."

Dov Dov walked over to the hole by the broken gate. He peered inside. There was something down there. Dov Dov put his hand in the hole. He pulled out something wet and soggy. It was a green leaf. An ordinary green leaf . . . and in it was a . . . chocolate-chip cookie.

Pajamas on Highway Ninety-Five

"Nothing exciting ever happens to us." Blimi sat in the backseat of their '69 Chevy-station wagon and grumbled.

Mrs. Silver answered from the front seat, "What would you like to happen?"

"I don't know."

Mrs. Silver said, "We're going to Monsey for *Shabbos* to visit Uncle Shmuel and Aunt Miriam."

"I know, but that's not exciting," Blimi insisted.

"But we'll see the new baby."

Elky sat between Blimi and Shragi. Blimi was nine. Elky was three years older.

"Don't you want to see them?" asked Shragi, who was three years younger than Blimi.

"Of course I do. I've been waiting for this trip for two months. I'm happy we're going. It's just that I'm bored. B-O-A-R-D bored!"

"That's not how you spell bored," Elky corrected her.

"Smarty," Blimi retorted.

"Look who's talking." Elky nudged her with her elbow.

"That's enough," Mr. Silver said, his voice firm. "Please let's have some peace and quiet until we get there. It's a long trip."

"What time is it, Mommy?" asked Blimi.

"It's seven-forty-five."

"How much longer, Mommy?" asked Shragi.

"We're only in Delaware. I'd say about three more hours."

BOOM! THUD!

"What was that?" all five passengers yelled.

"I don't know, but you'd better stop the car and check," said Mrs. Silver.

Mr. Silver pulled off the road as far as he could onto the gravel shoulder. It was dark. It was hard to see across the highway. Lights of speeding cars and trucks flashed quickly by.

"It's our suitcase!" Blimi heard Mrs. Silver moan. "It fell off the top of the car!"

"Where is it?" Blimi yelled.

"I don't know," said Mr. Silver. "You kids remain in the car. Mommy and I are going back to see if we can find it."

They took flashlights and began walking, being careful to stay on the shoulder. Blimi stared out the back window, together with Elky and Shragi. She looked at the dimness ahead and the blur of the road, and watched her parents moving further and further away.

"Well, Big Shot," snapped Elky. "You wanted something to happen and you got it."

Blimi was too scared to answer. All her clothing were in that suitcase, her *Shabbos* shoes, her favorite 'mentchies' with her doll furniture.

"What was that flying in the air?" Shragi asked. They peered ahead.

"It's my pajamas!" Blimi shrieked. "My pajamas!"

She stared horrified, as a truck zoomed by and ran over her pajamas. She watched in dreaded fascination at the incredible spectacle — her pajamas, flying up into the air, like a kite, then landing in shreds back on the highway.

As time passed, more and more of their belongings could be

seen flying by their window. Shirts, dresses, shoes, a man's suit, a tie. It was hard to make out the objects in the dark. Something that looked like an alarm clock crashed. Another crash; maybe it was their camera. A car or a truck would soon zoom over it and the article would waver and fly across the lanes.

Blimi saw this grotesque scene through a mist. It was a mist of salty tears that welled from smarting eyes and confusion. Blimi and Elky glanced at each other, Elky's eyes were wide and unbelieving. Blimi felt cold and afraid.

"This can't be happening!" She thought. "These things happen to other people. Not to us."

She felt sick and confused. Her stomach was churning, and her heart felt high in her throat.

Time had ceased to mean anything. Minute by minute, the night assumed greater aspects of gloom and despair.

The darkness bore down on Blimi with a weight she could feel. They were abandoned in the car. When would her parents return? Blimi felt cramped and half suffocated. She wished she could escape.

After what seemed like hours, her parents returned. "Well, that's that!" said Mrs. Silver breathless and shaky. "There's nothing we can do. It's too dangerous to run on to the highway to get what's left. And besides, there not much left. Everything is tattered into shreds."

Blimi tried to stop the sob that welled up inside of her. She covered her face with her hands. "My clothing!" she wailed.

"My new coat," said Elky.

"My teddy bear," cried Shragi.

Mrs. Silver turned around and faced them. Her face was white, but she spoke firmly and calmly. "*Baruch Hashem*, there was no accident. No one was hurt. *Zol zein a kaparah!*"

"*Zol zein a kaparah!*" agreed Mr. Silver.

"What does that mean?" Blimi asked.

"Well," said Mrs. Silver thoughtfully. "Sometimes *Hashem* wants something to happen to us; we don't know why. Maybe we did something wrong and He wants to wake us up to do *teshuvah*. But then, instead of making it happen to us, He gives us another chance and makes something else happen to our belongings instead."

"You mean like taking our clothing instead of our car?" asked Blimi.

"Maybe."

Blimi shuddered. She tried to understand what her parents were saying. But those were her pajamas out there on the highway. And it hurt to think she was never going to see her favorite "menchies" again.

Shragi began to cry. Blimi put her arm around him.

"Don't cry, Shragi. We'll buy you a new teddy bear. Right, Mommy?"

"Yes, dear, we'll need to do a lot of shopping when we get back to Baltimore."

Elky began to sing a soft, sweet *niggun*. Blimi joined her. Shragi smiled faintly. He put his head on Blimi's shoulder and was soon asleep.

※ ※ ※

The following morning Mr. Silver realized his *tefillin* were missing. "They were in the suitcase," he groaned. "Oh, no, my *tefillin!*" His shoulders drooped. It was too late to go back. *Shabbos* was starting early. He borrowed *tefillin* from Uncle

Shmuel but his heart was heavy. All *Shabbos,* he kept thinking, "My *tefillin!* My *tefillin!*"

Aunt Miriam borrowed clothing from her friends and their children, so everyone had what to wear. Blimi wore a pretty red and blue, flowered, lacy dress.

"It's prettier than mine," she told Elky. "But I'd still rather have my own dress."

"We all would," said Elky. "But remember what Mommy said, '*Zol zein a kaparah.*' "

"Yeah," said Blimi.

When the *Shabbos* candles were lit, Blimi felt a peacefulness and calm, despite her experience.

"*Shabbos* is here," said Mrs. Silver. "Let's all relax and enjoy the *Shabbos* peace."

Blimi held her new cousin and laughed when the baby gurgled and showed her toothless grin. She went to *shul*, played with her cousins, and sang *zemiros* during the *Shabbos* meals. It was a peaceful *Shabbos.* But when *Havdalah* was over and they got ready for their trip back to Baltimore, Blimi had a blurred memory of the details of Thursday night. It was like a miserable dream.

"My pajamas are laying out there, on the highway," she wailed.

"Be happy you aren't in them," Elky laughed.

The trip back to Baltimore was uneventful.

"Wait till I tell Bubby and Zaidy what happened," said Blimi.

"I wanna tell them," Shragi persisted.

"I want to!"

"No! I want to!"

"Here we go again," said Mrs. Silver.

❧ ❧ ❧

Bubby and Zaidy were sitting on the front porch when the station wagon pulled up in front of their house.

"Bubby! Zaidy!" Blimi ran up to them, almost tripping over her own feet.

"Blimele! *Kinderlach!*" Zaidy stood up and rushed over to them.

"Wait till . . ." Blimi began.

"Wait till I tell you what happened," Zaidy said before she finished.

Blimi stopped. "What happened to who?" She was puzzled.

Zaidy looked at them all. He seemed paler than usual, but his eyes held a soft glow.

"Thursday night," he began, "after you left, Bubby was going to a *shiur* in the Glen Avenue Shul. Oh — it must have been a quarter to eight, or so. Anyway, she was walking slowly, when all of a sudden — Oy, *Ribbono Shel Olam!*" He stopped and shook his head back and forth.

"What? Zaidy? What?" Blimi demanded.

"A car . . ." Zaidy found it hard to speak. "A car . . . went out of control . . . it drove up onto the sidewalk . . . right where Bubby was walking . . . and . . . and it missed her . . . by two feet."

Blimi was aghast! Bubby! CAR! Seven-forty-five! Her eyes stared horrified. Then as if woken up from a bad dream, she rushed to Bubby and hugged her with all her might.

"Oh, Bubby," she sobbed, her tears choking her.

"Mamele, don't cry," said Bubby. "Look, see, I'm all right."

Blimi continued hugging her and crying. "Oh, Bubby, I love you so much more than my pajamas."

A few weeks later, on the last night of *Chanukah*, Blimi was watching her father get the *Chanukah menorah* ready. There was a knock on the door.

"I'll get it," she shouted.

Everyone followed her. She opened the door. A tall dark boy, about eighteen years old, wearing a black leather jacket, was standing there. His motorcycle was parked in front of the house.

Blimi gaped at him. He looked tired and dirty, but he had a nice face. He stared. They stared at him. He seemed tongue tied. When he spoke his words flooded out in disorder.

"Um . . . I . . . uh . . ." he stammered. "Well you see, it's . . . like this . . .uh . . . in Delaware . . . uh . . . a few weeks ago, Highway ninety-five, I saw this strange object on the side of the road. I went to check it and I uh . . . it . . . was this. It had your name and address on it, and everything."

Mr. Silver's mouth popped open. "My *tefillin!*" he boomed.

"I . . . uh . . . remembered," continued the boy, "I used to see stuff like this when I visited my grandparents. I know it's something religious."

Mr. Silver was the first to speak. "Oh, thank you so much. What is your name?"

"Jeff, Jeff Steinberg."

"Jeff, you can't imagine how happy you have made us. Won't you come in?"

And Jeff came in just in time for lighting the *Chanukah menorah.*

Good-bye, Mrs. Kay

urry up, Taibele. Everybody's waiting."

"Mmmm-mmmm," mumbled Taibele, pointing to her *siddur*. She still wasn't finished *davening*. It's not that it took her much longer to *daven* than the other girls. It's just that she had just made a discovery. She was amazed.

"Imagine," she thought, "I'm going to be saying *Atah vechartanu* now, in *Shemoneh Esrei,* and I won't be saying it again for almost six more months. Imagine that."

She continued being amazed. "It's not like the everyday *Shemoneh Esrei*, or even the *Shabbos Shemoneh Esrei*. We say *Atah vechartanu*, only five times a year, on *Rosh Hashanah, Yom Kippur, Succos, Pesach,* and *Shavuos.*" Now it was *Simchas Torah* and the next time she would be saying it would be *Pesach;* six whole months away. What a mind-shaking thought.

She would say it slowly and clearly, with a lot of *kavanah*. After all, six months was a long time away. "*Atah vechartanu mikal ha'amim* — You have chosen us from all other nations."

"TAIBELE!"

"Mmmmm-mmmm."

After ten more minutes, Taibele called to her mother. "Good-bye, Mom, I'm going to the old-age home now. The girls are waiting outside for me."

"O.K., Mamele, have a nice time. Did you *daven*?"

"Yup."

"Did you remember to say *mashiv haruach?*"

"Uh . . . oh . . . well . . . I . . . n . . . no!"

"Whoops, you'd better go *daven Shemoneh Esrei* again, dear."

"How about that?" said Taibele. "Here I thought I wouldn't be saying *Atah vechartanu* again for six months, and now it's only ten minutes later and I'm saying it again."

Taibele finished *davening* for the second time and the girls began their long walk to the old-age home. The air was brisk with the chill of autumn. Taibele never lost her sense of wonder at the beauty around her.

The leaves were shining with their brilliant colors.

"Aaahh!" Taibele took a deep breath.

She looked at a reddish-orange leaf, lines running through it like delicate veins.

There were so many beautiful things out there in the world, so many happy, good things. If only she could package some and give it to Mrs. Kay as a gift.

"You sure took a long time," said Malky.

"Yeah, I'm sorry. It's hard to explain."

"Look," said Shaindy, "I'm bringing these cookies that I baked for Mr. Blackman."

"I'm bringing this book to Mrs. Grossberg," said Zahava.

"I have lots of stories to tell Mrs. Kay," said Taibele.

"Mrs. Kay?" repeated all three girls. "You mean Mrs. Grumpy."

"Yeah, but I don't call her that."

"Well, why do you always visit her, Taibele? She's no fun at all," said Malky.

"Yeah," agreed Zahava, "when I speak to her, she never seems to pay any attention and has a grumpy look on her face. She never smiles or talks or even nods her head like Mrs. Grossberg."

"I know," said Taibele, skipping along to catch up with the other girls. "It's just that . . . I don't know, I think she's more lonely than the others. She never has any visitors or company. No one ever talks to her. She seems so alone in the world. I feel sorry for her."

"But she doesn't appreciate anything you do for her," said Chavi logically.

"Yeah! How do you know she even understands you?" asked Malky

"I know she understands me," said Taibele with a slight toss of her head, "and I think she does appreciate it even though she doesn't show it."

"Well, you can waste your time if you want," said Chavi, "but I've got plenty of people to visit who do appreciate me," she said with finality.

The home was crowded. A stooped man smiled and dipped his head in recognition. Another man peered at her through pale-rimmed glasses.

"Hello, Mr. Shuman," said Taibele.

The girls separated and each went her own way to bring some joy and comfort to the lonely inhabitants of the home.

Taibele searched for Mrs. Kay. She walked through the long clean halls, the walls white and shiny like a hospital. Taibele soon spotted Mrs. Kay sitting in a corner by a window. She was wearing a faded blue cotton dress. Her feet were covered with brown furry slippers. She looks like a statue, thought Taibele, an old stone statue.

"Hi, Mrs. Kay," called Taibele, cheerfully. "Sorry I'm late, but it's hard to explain. How are you doing?"

Mrs. Kay looked at Taibele, her face looked like a mask of finely

creased leather. She showed no sign of recognition. Taibele continued, undaunted. "I hope you don't mind that I keep calling you Mrs. Kay. Mrs. Kaminezovski is a real nice name too. It's not that I don't like it," she chattered on, "it's just that Mrs. Kay is much shorter and easier to say. It takes less time, so I could have more time to talk about other things. Oh, here I go again, rattling on and on. I hope you don't mind."

Taibele took a chair and stood it opposite Mrs. Kay so she could look straight into her face. She made herself comfortable.

"I bet when you were younger, you were real busy, with lots of kids. I bet you had to work real hard to cook and clean and iron your husband's shirts. My mother says I'm a big help but I'd be even a bigger help if I'd speak a little less and work a little more."

Taibele paused to catch her breath and take a large gulp. It was

difficult to get Mrs. Kay to react to anything with even the mildest enthusiasm. She showed almost no curiosity about anything. Taibele sighed.

"You know what happened last week on the way to school?" She laughed at the thought. "There we were, my mother in the front of the car with me, and four girls in the back, when suddenly! Whammo! Flat tire! There we were, stuck with no way to get to school and no one to help us. We had a spare tire in the trunk of the car, but my mother didn't know how to fix it. Cars kept honking at us and were angry that we were slowing down traffic. Oy."

Taibele's eyes sparkled with merriment, and laughter began to tumble from her throat.

"Then, suddenly, out of the clear blue sky, this man stops his car, and says, 'Good morning, ladies, can I be of help?' And quick

Good-bye, Mrs. Kay / 29

as a wink, or more like twenty minutes, he jacked up the car, fixed our tire and was off. We didn't even know his name. As he started to drive away, my mother called, "Please, sir, can't I pay you?' But he just said, 'Lady, do a favor to someone else who's in a pickle someday, and it'll be like you're paying me back. That's what makes the world go round.' And he drove away."

Taibele seemed to run down like a clock that needed winding. She talked on and on, chatting and laughing, telling her funny stories and comments. She remembered the leaf she had put in her pocket during *Chol Hamoed*. "Look, Mrs. Kay. Look at this beautiful leaf. The streets are full of them. Orange, red, gold, yellow. It looks like a dazzling painting flashing through the sky. Maybe we can take a walk outside and look at them. You'll like that."

She handed the leaf to the old woman. Mrs. Kay looked up at her with searching eyes. Her head tilted to one side. Her body moved a little forward. Slowly, very slowly, she opened her mouth as if to speak. Her mouth twitched and her eyebrows lifted in a quizzical expression. Then she closed her mouth again and the moment was gone.

Taibele's heart was swollen with compassion. She longed to say some comforting words to Mrs. Kay.

"She looks so sad and lonely," thought Taibele. "I wish I could take some of the happiness from inside of me and put it into her."

Taibele stood up and reached down to plant a kiss on Mrs. Kay's cheek.

Mrs. Kay looked up with a helpless air about her.

"Good-bye, Mrs. Kay. I'll see you next week. Don't go away. O.K.?" Taibele laughed, rushing off, her black braids sailing behind her. "Good-bye, Mrs. Kay."

Three days later, Taibele received a call from the home. Was it possible for her to come right away? Mrs. Kay hadn't been feeling well and had asked for her.

"She asked for me?" Taibele was stunned. "She actually spoke and asked for me?"

"Yes," said her mother, driving her to the home. "That was what the superintendent at the home said. She clearly asked for 'Taibele'."

"I can't believe it!"

Taibele felt awkward walking down the halls of the home without her friends. The halls seemed different at night, quieter, more deserted and abandoned. She could smell the antiseptic scent of the white spotless floors.

The halls seemed endless. Rooms, rooms and more rooms. Nurses walked back and forth. Occasionally a visitor came out of a room.

"Here we are," said the nurse who had accompanied her. "You can go right in."

Mrs. Kay's door was partly opened. Taibele walked in quietly. Mrs. Kay lay on her bed. Her face was drawn and pale. She seemed to be asleep. Taibele's eyes swept the dimly lit room with a searching glance, then she studied Mrs. Kay silently. Taibele approached the old woman.

"Mrs. Kay," she whispered quietly.

The old woman's eyes fluttered open and looked at her. Were the lips twitching into a smile?

"Hi, Mrs. Kay," said Taibele. "You asked me to come?"

A slight nod. The old hand slowly lifted and pointed to the dresser. Taibele followed the move. On the dresser was a picture. She picked it up. She studied the picture in her hands. From within the frame a face looked back at Taibele. The face was that of a girl of about ten or eleven years old. Twinkling brown eyes looked out from a slim pointed face. Dark straight hair was parted in the middle and drawn into two thick braids. The girl was laughing.

"Who is this?" asked Taibele. "Is this you when you were little, or your little girl, or your grandchild?"

Mrs. Kay pointed with her bony finger to herself, then to the picture, then to Taibele. She mumbled something.

"What?"

The words were barely audible.

"For you."

Taibele understood.

"You want me to keep the picture? Oh, thank you, thank you so much." She felt a lump in her throat.

"I'll always treasure it." Taibele nearly choked on the words.

Mrs. Kay motioned for Taibele to come closer. She was mumbling and her words were barely above a whisper. Taibele put her face closer to Mrs. Kay. Her voice sounded far away.

"You . . . have . . . made . . . me . . . happy . . . child . . . and . . . you . . . have . . . a loving . . . heart."

Suddenly, like a morning sunrise, a smile spread across the wrinkled old face; a smile that grew and blossomed till her whole being seemed to take on a look of pure joy.

"I'm happy," answered Taibele. She felt hot tears on her cheeks.

"I'm happy I've made you happy. But you know what, Mrs. Kay? You're the one who's made me happy." She bent closer and kissed Mrs. Kay's cheek. It felt soft as velvet.

"I love you, Mrs. Kay."

Mrs. Kay closed her eyes, the smile still set. Taibele felt a bond between the old woman and herself. She tiptoed to the door. She turned back. She stood rigidly. Her eyes took in every detail of the figure lying on the bed. She gave one last lingering look. The figure on the bed was still, her face peaceful and contented. Taibele closed the door softly.

"Good-bye, Mrs. Kay."

Partners Forever

Mendy stood looking up at the stone building. Thoughts and memories flashed through his mind like an old reel of film. "It's been a long time," thought Mendy, "a very long time . . ."

❦ ❦ ❦

Mendy and Shaya were best friends. They had been best friends for years and years; in fact, ever since they had known each other. Of course they didn't know each other until they knew each other. That is, they were both born on the same day and lived next door to each other. They took their first steps together even though Mendy walked four months earlier but Shaya made up for it by speaking six months earlier than Mendy.

The two boys had done almost everything together. It had been sort of a joke around town about the two un-look-a-like twins who were always seen together. Even though the two were very different in looks, their personalities complimented each other.

Mendy was the taller of the two. He was dark and husky with twinkling eyes and a mischievous grin. He loved sports, any kind, and was usually captain when teams were chosen. Shaya was fair and quiet. He had intelligent brown eyes and enjoyed thinking about things.

When the boys started first grade, Shaya was too shy to make friends and it was Mendy who took him into the crowd.

It was Mendy who taught Shaya how to swing a bat, ride a bike, and swim like a fish. But it was Shaya who taught Mendy how to read, helped him with his *Chumash* and his multiplication tables.

During the summer months the boys went to sleep-away camp and even there they stuck together.

"I don't understand!" people used to say, "They're so different yet they seem to enjoy each other so much."

It was there that Mendy taught Shaya how to swim.

"I'm scared," Shaya said. The water was cold and he shivered. "Be my partner, Mendy. Don't let me drown!"

"You won't drown. I'll hold you." With care and skill Mendy showed Shaya the swim strokes and helped him overcome his fear of the water.

Mendy also taught Shaya how to ride a bike.

"I'm going to fall!"

"No you're not!" Mendy said, "I won't let you."

Shaya leaned over the handle bars and pumped as hard as he could. He looked straight ahead and tore down the street, Mendy running with him. "Yippee! I can do it! I can do it!" shouted Shaya, triumphantly, the wind blowing in his face.

It was Shaya who helped Mendy when Mendy had trouble in school. "I'll never learn how to read!" Mendy had said in first grade.

"Sure you will!" said Shaya, and with unusual patience and understanding Shaya practiced and practiced with Mendy till Mendy knew how to read as well as anyone in the class. And when Mendy had trouble a few years later with the times tables, Shaya again came to his aid.

When Mendy had trouble grasping *Chumash* and *Rashi* it was Shaya who explained the lessons to him over and over again.

So it went. Where one boy was weak, the other boy was strong;

and that was how they complemented each other.

Shaya was a great storyteller and often Mendy would beg, "C'mon, Shaya, make up a story for me!" And Shaya would begin weaving his tales on long lazy summer afternoons while Mendy sat transfixed.

When things would get boring, Mendy — a great seeker of adventure — would take Shaya on hikes through the woods and hills to hidden caves. He told Shaya funny jokes till Shaya had tears in his eyes from laughing.

In school, on all the trips, the boys were always partners. There was the time the boys went on a class trip to Washington, D.C., and wandered off and got lost. It was Shaya, with his keen sense of direction, who led the boys back to the school bus.

"Mendy, let's always be partners," Shaya said. Mendy slapped Shaya's hand hard and laughed. "Sure, pal! We'll be partners forever."

The boys were often getting into trouble, thanks mostly to Mendy. There was the time they found a stray sheep dog they named Shtinky, which followed them to school.

"Here, Shtinky, you wait by the door and we'll pick you up after school. Now don't go away." Shtinky licked Shaya's face and almost knocked him down. He waited patiently during most of the morning until someone opened the front door. Then chaos broke loose. Mendy and Shaya's teacher opened the classroom door and some white flash made a gigantic leap and sailed onto the teacher. The teacher staggered and fell against the desk. Shtinky roared through the school halls and the boys followed like a herd of stampeding elephants.

If not for Mendy, Shaya would sit in front of a book the whole day. "Let's play basketball," Mendy said.

"Not now, I'm reading," Shaya answered, as he pressed his glasses back.

"Oh, c'mon, you can read later," Mendy said.

"Oh, all right!" Shaya would give in and the two would run and jump and shoot baskets. Mendy always won, but Shaya didn't mind. Mendy was fun to be with — and besides, Shaya figured, he always won when they played Checkers and Scrabble.

If not for Shaya, Mendy would be playing all day.

"C'mon, Mendy," Shaya would say, "we have to study *Gemara* for our test tomorrow."

"Not now," said Mendy, throwing the ball up, "maybe later."

Shaya grabbed the ball and ran away with it. Mendy ran and caught up with Shaya and the two boys fell on the grass panting, laughing and wrestling. Mendy would give in and struggle while Shaya, with his logic and clear thinking, explained the *Gemara* to him till he would know it. In this way, Mendy would get in the eighties on his tests. Shaya, of course, almost always got a hundred.

"You're so smart," said Mendy, "I betcha someday you're going to be a great big *Rosh Yeshiva* and I'll say 'I taught that *Rosh Yeshiva* how to play basketball.'"

Shaya laughed.

"And me," said Mendy, "I'm going to be a pilot and fly a super-sonic jet."

"You said you were going to be a drummer," Shaya pointed out.

"That was last week," Mendy explained.

During recess, Mendy would bring toys or rocks or anything he could find from home and sell them. He was a wheeler-dealer, and quickly sold his items. He shared his money with Shaya and

Partners Forever / 37

the two would stop on the way home from school and buy ice cream or soda.

The boys shared everything together, good times as well as troubled times. There was the time the boys had a caterpillar collection. The boys collected ninety-seven different kinds of caterpillars and hid them in a box in Shaya's bedroom under the bed. "Look, Mendy! There's a big red and green furry-looking one! I've never seen one like that!"

"Hey, that's neat!" said Mendy. He put his face close to the caterpillar. "Hi, fella, you look like my brother."

"And look!" said Shaya. "There's the fattest, furriest red caterpillar I've ever seen. Why, I bet we've got the biggest caterpillar collection in the whole wide world."

And maybe they would have, if Shaya's little brother hadn't opened the box, and let all the caterpillars escape all over the house.

"What's this?" shrieked Shaya's mother, as she almost stepped on a green and yellow something that was crawling on the kitchen floor. It took the boys two weeks to find all the caterpillars.

"I still don't think it was fair that we had to set them free in the woods," Mendy complained. "Hey, maybe we can start a spider collection!"

"I doubt my mother would let," said Shaya sadly.

Then there was the time the boys built a tree house in Mendy's backyard.

"This is great!" Mendy said. It was raining hard and the boys sat huddled in their cozy shelter. "We can stay here forever, partner," Shaya said. "We could bring games and food and even sleep here. Hey, Mendy — watch out!" Shaya called frantically. He heard the sound of ripping cloth.

Partners Forever / 39

Mendy's foot slipped on a wet board and he slid down the tree. "Help!"

It was Shaya who comforted Mendy during the two weeks Mendy had to stay in bed with a broken foot. Shaya played games with him and kept him company. He moved in for the two weeks and slept in a bed next to Mendy's.

"Shaya, you're my very best friend in the whole wide world."

"And you're mine, too, Mendy."

When the boys started high school, they weren't always in the same classes, but they still felt very close to each other. At their graduation both Shaya and Mendy won awards.

They sat spellbound with their eyes glued to the principal.

" . . . And now the Milton Beck award for outstanding diligence and effort in all his learning goes to Shaya Perlstein."

There was loud applause, the loudest coming from Mendy who started cheering and whistling till he got a stern look from one of the teachers.

" . . . And now," continued the principal, "the Judah Rand *Bein Adam Lachaveiro* award for the boy who showed true *chesed* and *lev tov* — Mendy Berman." Again loud cheering and clapping. But Shaya's face shone the brightest, with an expression of true pride in his best friend.

Then the inevitable came. After the boys graduated, for the first time in their lives, the boys were going to be separated.

Shaya was going to *Eretz Yisrael* to learn in a *yeshiva* there and Mendy was going to a *yeshiva* in the Midwest.

"I can't believe it, Shaya. What am I going to do without you?" said Mendy.

"And what am I going to do without you?" Shaya retorted.

The boys were spending their last evening home together. For the very first time in their lives they were to experience being on their own.

"I'm going to miss you so much." Shaya choked back tears.

"Will you write me often?" Mendy asked.

"I'll try," Shaya said.

"And I'll try to send you packages of food," Mendy said. "If I know anyone going to *Eretz Yisrael,* I'll ask him to bring a jar of peanut butter and some chocolate candy for you."

Shaya tried to say thank you, but the words caught in his throat.

"Do you think . . ." began Mendy. He stopped.

"Do I think what?"

"Do you think we'll always be best friends?"

"I know I'll always remember you and think of you as my best friend, Mendy."

"And I'll always think of you too," Mendy said, "especially at test times."

The boys laughed. It was a bittersweet laugh.

The parting the next day was quick. With both families around, there wasn't much time for private words. And before they realized it, they were parted.

At first, the boys wrote to each other and kept up a correspondence. They saw each other every *Succos* and *Pesach* when Shaya came home for the *Yomim Tovim*.

Years passed. Shaya married and lived in *Eretz Yisrael.* Mendy married, too, and lived in America. Mendy became a businessman. He was known for his wit, sharpness and capabilities. Good fortune shone on him. He became a rich man. With his money and capabilities he became an even richer man, until he far exceeded his own dreams. He was healthy, strong and ambitious. He lived in a comfortable home with his wife and four children.

And, to be sure, he gave much *tzedakah* and was a benefactor of any needy cause that came his way.

But Mendy felt that something was missing from his life. To outsiders he seemed happy and contented, but inside of him, Mendy felt an emptiness and loneliness, a craving for something — he did not know what. It was with these thoughts that Mendy said to his wife, Baila, "I've just got to have a change of scenery. Perhaps I should take a trip to Israel to visit my friend Shaya. It's been so many years since I've seen him."

"I think that's a wonderful idea," said Baila. "I've been after you for years to take a vacation. You work much too hard."

And so it was settled. As Mendy made preparations for his trip, his mood turned to excitement. He hadn't seen Shaya for so many years. He was always planning to visit his old friend, but he felt too pressured by his business to leave.

Mendy arrived in the Holy Land and was immediately spellbound by the beauty. The air seemed saturated with *kedushah*. He took a cab to Shaya's address. As the cab approached closer and closer, Mendy felt an eagerness and excitement that he hadn't felt for years.

❧ ❧ ❧

He stood now looking up at the stone building.

❧ ❧ ❧

"Mendy!" shouted a figure running out of the house. Mendy blinked and brought his mind back from a long way off.

"Shaya?" Mendy didn't recognized his old friend at first. He had a long beard, and he seemed thinner and older. "It's been so long."

Shaya laughed and Mendy recognized the sparkle in his best friend's eyes. They hugged each other, and suddenly they felt that time hadn't passed for them. It was as if they had been together all these past years. The same familiarity and closeness was there.

"Oh, it's good to set eyes on you again," Mendy said, as the two walked into the house.

"Come in, come in. Shaindy, look who's here!"

"What a beautiful bunch!" Mendy exclaimed. Shaya swelled with pride.

"This is Devoiry. She's ten. Chezky, nine. Shmulie, seven. Simmie, five. Mendy, four. Shanie, three. Rochie, two. And Berel, he's almost one."

The children looked on shyly. Their eyes were wide with curiosity. Mendy loved them immediately. Oh, it was so good to be together with Shaya again!

For the next few days Mendy stayed and ate at Shaya's house, and came to realize how great a *talmid chacham* Shaya had become. The children loved Mendy and fought with each other over who got to sit on his lap. Mendy told them funny stories and jokes, and Shaya looked on with amusement. "Partner," said Mendy, "you haven't changed at all. Behind that black beard and big glasses hides the same little Shaya I always knew. The same kind, understanding, brilliant *boychik* that I remember!"

Shaya laughed, "You haven't changed much either, Mendy. And *Baruch Hashem* for that!"

On the last night before Mendy was leaving, he was upset. He had heard some very disturbing news.

"Why didn't you tell me, Shaya?" he asked.

"Tell you what?"

For the first time Mendy took a good look at the poverty Shaya's family lived in. The over-crowded rooms, the shabby furniture, the torn clothing the children wore.

"Tell you what?" Shaya repeated.

Mendy was distressed.

"Rabbi Wolff told me you were leaving the *yeshiva* to look for a job."

Shaya lowered his head.

Mendy continued, "He said you were having a very hard time making ends meet, and now you can barely feed your family. Is that true, Shaya?"

Shaya lifted his head. "It's true," he said softly.

Mendy was aghast. Shaya leave the *yeshiva?* But that was terrible. Shaya was a promising future *gadol*. How could he let this happen! Then suddenly, like a light at the end of a tunnel, Mendy knew and understood what to do.

"Shaya," he began. "You've been honest with me. Please let me be honest with you."

Shaya looked puzzled but remained silent.

"For a long time now," Mendy began, "I've been feeling depressed and unhappy with myself. My business is flourishing and I have everything I could possibly want. But I've been feeling an emptiness and uselessness with my life. What is the purpose? I wake up every day, eat, work, sleep, and work some more, but where is it getting me? Now it just hit me what is wrong. Shaya, I've never had your brains, but more than that I've always been too restless to sit and learn all day. Business affords me the opportunity to run around and exert my energy, but I felt it was wrong. What was I doing for my Torah life? What good is all the money I'm making if I can't use it for Torah?"

Mendy's eyes lit up. "Shaya, do you remember when we learned about Yissachar and Zevulun, Yaakov's two sons?"

"They were partners," said Shaya.

"That's right!" said Mendy, excitedly. "Zevulun worked hard and supported Yissachar so that Yissachar would learn Torah all day without worrying about money needs. That way, Yissachar's Torah became Zevulun's Torah too."

He stopped and looked Shaya straight in the eyes. His voice was full of emotion. He whispered, "Shaya, will you be my Yissachar?"

Shaya couldn't speak. Suddenly his eyes shone and the old twinkle returned. "Yes, Zevulun. Thank you."

The two best friends embraced. Then Mendy shook Shaya's hand heartily. "Now, we'll really be partners — partners forever."

Tornado Alert

Batya was more scared that she had ever been in her life. It must have been hours since her father and her mother had left for the hospital. Her mother was going to have a baby. Batya was baby-sitting for her younger two brothers, Yanky, eight, and Donny, two. Mrs. Klein, her next door neighbor was supposed to have come, but she had never arrived.

It was just a minute or two after Batya heard the warning on the radio. "TORNADO ALERT! TORNADO ALERT! This is a civil defense emergency!"

Batya had lived in Atlanta for all her ten years and she had never experienced a real honest-to-goodness tornado.

"I'd love to see one," Yanky said.

"Are you nuts?" Batya asked. "Do you realize what that would mean?"

She shuddered at the thought, and now, here she was all alone with her two brothers. The phone was dead. The radio was dead. She had no contact with the outside world.

"What are we going to do, Batya?" asked Yanky. "Let's get Donny out of the crib," said Batya, "and we'll go down to the basement and sit under the doorposts."

"But Donny's sleeping. You know what he's like when you try to wake him up."

"I know, but there's no choice. C'mon, we've got to take cover fast."

Batya rushed up two flights of stairs. Donny was sleeping,

holding his worn teddy bear. He whined and grumbled as Batya frantically woke him and carried him out of the room. She turned back. She grabbed his teddy bear, two diapers, and his woolen blanket. And here they were now, sitting in this stuffy basement, an eerie light shining from the bare bulb in the hall.

"I wonder if Mommy had the baby." Yanky asked. "I hope it's a boy."

"I'd like a sister."

"What's going to happen to us, Batya?" asked Yanky.

"We'll be O.K.," answered Batya, with more confidence than she felt.

"Do you think Daddy and Mommy made it to the hospital before the tornado alarm sounded?"

"How should I know? And stop asking me so many questions. I've got my hands full trying to keep Donny happy."

She had used up the two diapers and she needed more. Why hadn't she thought to bring down the whole box? It was a good thing Yanky had thought to bring down Donny's pacifier. She gave it to him now. He rested his head on her shoulder. She felt him relax.

She looked around the basement. She could see the posters on the wall above her father's desk.

"Silence is golden." Yes, she knew that one.

"Hang in there." Hang in where?

"Don't judge a book by its cover." Why not?

"Keep things in the right per . . . spec . . . tive." She wasn't really sure what that meant. Something about realizing what things really were important.

She could see her desk and toyshelves, her favorite dolls, her books, her bicycle, and her rock collection. They were all there.

Her jewelry! The silver ring her grandmother had sent for her birthday.

And her most prized possession in the whole world, her doll house. Her father had built it for her. It had taken him weeks to build it. How she loved it! She loved it more than anything in the world. She stared again at her doll house with the little blue curtain in the tiny window and the little red chimney made out of real bricks. And now it might get ruined. Why, the whole house could crumble and collapse.

Why, they all might get killed!

What difference did it make if her old doll-house got destroyed when their very lives were at stake? Who cared about an old doll-house?

Batya looked at Yanky, hunched over with a frown on his face. Donny was sleeping, his face flushed but peaceful. Batya felt a tremendous rush of love for her two brothers. How could she care about an old doll-house at a time like this?

What was that word over her father's desk? Per . . . spec . . . tive. Doesn't that mean everything in its order of importance? And what could be more important now than she and her brothers remaining safe. How unimportant everything else seemed. Her doll house, her toys, everything in the house — what was their purpose? Per . . . spec . . . tive!

Suddenly, she heard the chilling sound of a siren screeching. The lights started flickering on and off, on and off.

"What's that awful sucking sound?" Yanky asked. It was coming from the drains in the pipe. Batya felt an awful pulling in her ears, like vacuums were pulling at them from both ends.

The tornado was getting close. Both her ears popped and then there was a lull of deadly quiet. Batya felt a tremendous heat; she found it difficult to breathe. Above them they could hear the furniture moving and crashing along the floor. Crack! A window broke. Another and another. Shattered glass was everywhere.

"Get under the blankets!" Batya screamed. She took Donny's blanket and covered them all. A heavy pressure filled the room; it felt like something was trying to lift them off the floors. They lay huddled together under the doorpost.

A tremendous roar like jet planes filled the air. The sound of the wind filled the room, roaring, humming, howling, shrieking. Then it stopped.

"I . . . is it over?" Yanky whimpered.

"I . . . d . . . don't . . . know." Batya's teeth were chattering. It began to hail. Big marble-size hailstones were pouring down, hitting them like bullets. Batya covered her brothers with her own body. She kept thinking about her mother and father. Did they make it to the hospital in time, before the tornado hit?

"Please, *Hashem*," she *davened*. Her lips moved but she couldn't hear her own words. "Please give us our lives. Don't let anything happen to us. Take care of Yanky and Donny and me, and Mommy and Daddy. I'll try to always . . . (she thought of the poster on the basement wall) . . . keep things in the right perspective."

The storm continued to rage, like an enemy, ready to devour and destroy. Batya shivered with cold and fright. "*Hashem* help us! Help us! Help us!" she repeated over and over again.

Water was gurgling and splashing on the basement floor. The noise rumbled to a high pitch. Thunder crashed and boomed. Lightning flashed. Then it stopped.

Batya heard the sirens wail. She didn't know how much time had passed. It seemed like the end of the world.

Suddenly, a light appeared above them. "Anybody down there?" called a familiar shaky voice.

"Daddy! Daddy!" Batya thought. She was screaming but the voice came out in a frightened whisper. Her body shook with uncontrollable sobs. She experienced such an enormous feeling of relief that her head reeled dizzily.

Her father was hugging them all tightly. Batya felt like her bones were crunching. She wished her father would hold her like this forever and never let her go.

"Oh, Batya," he cried. There were heavy shadows under his eyes and a hoarseness in his voice. "You can't imagine what we went through when we got to the hospital and we heard about the tornado alert. I couldn't get back to you. The police wouldn't let anyone back into the danger zone. I can't tell you what a nightmare it was, waiting till they let me return."

Her father was crying. She had never seen her father cry.

"Daddy, don't cry, we're all O.K. — see?"

"Yes, Batya, yes, I see," her father said. "*Baruch Hashem.* You're all O.K. Nothing else matters, just that you're all safe."

PERSPECTIVE! The word flashed through Batya's mind.

"Hey, Daddy!" Yanky asked, wiping his eyes with his grimy hands. "Did Mommy have a baby?"

Batya had completely forgotten. It seemed like such a long time ago. She held her breath.

"Yes, *Mazel Tov!*" Her father smiled a broad grin from ear to ear. "You now have a new baby brother."

"A brother!"

Her father's smile seemed to stretch wider and wider. "AND . . . A NEW BABY SISTER."

Watch out Below

Whenever Leeba saw the dazzling lights of the amusement park she felt excited. Once a year her class went on a trip to Adventureland.

"I've been waiting so long for this trip," said Chedva, a dark-haired girl with bright eyes.

"Me too," said Leeba, her heavy-fringed hazel eyes shining. "I love all the rides: the roller coaster, the moonjump, the scrambler, the Ferris wheel."

"My mother gave me three dollars to spend," said Chedva.

"I also have three dollars," said Leeba. "But I don't know what to buy."

"Let's first go on the rides. Then we'll stop at the souvenir store and choose something."

"O.K."

"Hey, Chedva, Leeba!" Malky called. "Are you coming with us? We're going on the Ferris wheel." Tova, Shaindy and Judy were waiting with them.

"Sure," said Chedva.

The girls were running around laughing and shrieking.

"Chedva, look!" said Leeba. She pointed to a nearby tree where a lone figure stood.

"It's Ella. What about her?"

"She's all alone," Chedva pointed out.

"I know," Leeba said, "but now it's much worse. Everybody is busy having so much fun together and no one is staying with her."

Malky overheard her. "Well, you know Ella. You can't have much fun with her. She's such a stick in the mud."

"Let's just go ask her if she wants to join us," suggested Leeba.

"Uh-uh, not me," said Tova. "If she sticks with us, nobody's going to have fun. She's so slow and she talks funny too," said Shaindy.

"What's that got to do with anything?" Leeba was getting upset. "It's not her fault she's slow and what difference does it make how she talks. She still has feelings, just like you and me."

"Well, you do what you want," said Malky. "We didn't come here to have a dumb time. We're going on the Ferris wheel now. C'mon, Chedva, let's go."

Chedva looked at Malky. Then she looked back at Leeba. She looked at Ella standing all alone. She made up her mind.

"I'm going with Leeba and Ella," she said with finality. Leeba smiled at her. Good old Chedva. She knew she could count on her. She took her hand and together the two girls approached Ella.

"Hi, Ella," said Leeba and Chedva.

"Hi," Ella said shyly.

"Want to come with us on the rides?"

"Oh . . . th-th-thank you." Ella's face lit up.

"We're going on the Ferris wheel," said Chedva.

"Th-the Ferris wheel?"

"Yeah, you know the big wheel that turns around."

"Oh no!" Ella opened her eyes wide. "I can't."

"Why not?"

"I'm too scared to go on that ride."

"Don't worry," said Chedva. "We'll go with you. You'll like it."

But Ella shook her head emphatically. "No, no, I can't go on that."

Leeba was beginning to wonder if the other girls had been right. "Well, what do you want to go on?" she asked.

Ella smiled. "I love the merry-go-round." Chedva and Leeba exchanged glances.

"O.K.," said Leeba. "Let's go on the merry-go-round first." She was hoping that maybe Ella would change her mind.

Long lines of children stood at the ticket booth waiting eagerly for their turn. Dozens of girls were clamoring to ride the Ferris wheel.

Leeba looked up at the Ferris wheel. The cars were rising and turning, going up, going down, steadily. She could hear the clankings of the roller chains in their sprockets. It was her favorite ride. The Ferris wheel was moving now at its ordained top speed and the rim flashed past her fascinated gaze. The tip of the curving crescent grew close.

Leeba looked at the girls up there with nothing below them but empty air. The girls were floating quietly above their surroundings. When they were halfway up, the wheels stopped as another car was loaded.

Leeba was amazed at the soundlessness and smoothness of the great mass of steel.

"Let's go on the Ferris wheel," she pleaded.

"No, please," said Ella, her voice shaking and scared.

After going on the merry-go-round two more times, Leeba had enough.

"Let's stop at the souvenir shop," she said. She was beginning to regret her decision. Then she looked at Ella's happy face. She was bursting with excitement. Leeba felt ashamed of herself.

At the souvenir shop they looked at the dazzling display of dolls, books, pictures and games. Chedva bought a small sailor hat. Leeba wanted a small wooden dog. It looked so sad and lovable. Ella had her eyes glued on a picture of a clown.

"Oh!" She laughed. "I wish I had that picture."

"Do you have any money?" Leeba asked.

"No." Ella laughed. "Oh, it's so funny. I have no pictures of clowns. I love it." She jumped up and down and clapped her hands.

Leeba looked at the little wooden puppy. She looked at the clown. She had other animals at home. Big stuffy, warm animals. Teddy bears, dogs, kittens, monkeys. What did she need a wooden dog for? But Ella had no clowns. Leeba took one last look at the puppy.

"I'll take the picture of the clown." she said loudly.

She paid for it and gave it to Ella.

"For m-m-me?!" Ella smiled her crooked smile. "My funny clown." She giggled and held the picture tightly to her.

GROAN-SQUEAK-CREAK. The girls rushed out of the store to see what the commotion was about. They heard scraping and rattling. Chedva had a sickly look on her face.

Leeba stared and froze in terror. She could see Malky up on the Ferris wheel. The unsupported weight of the car caved and began to sag and bend.

There was confusion as screaming and crying filled her ears. Leeba's face was ashen. She put her hands to her face and broke out in heartbroken weeping. She shivered from head to foot. Her heart beat wildly with fear.

Men were running in all directions. Ella was clutching her arms, her fingers digging into herself. Chedva looked like she was going to faint.

The sound of sirens could be heard. Ambulances came, fire

Watch out Below / 57

engines. It all happened so fast. It seemed unreal. Leeba watched in terror. Everything swam as though a window streaming with rain interrupted her view.

The trip back home was a sober one. Leeba sat with Chedva and Ella. No one spoke. It was only after Leeba came home and fell into her mother's arms that she let herself sob and cry loudly, and told her mother all about the accident.

Leeba's mother immediately called the hospital. After completing the call, she pressed Leeba close to her. "They'll all be back to normal pretty soon, a few broken bones and sprained ankles, but nothing worse and nothing that won't heal, *Baruch Hashem*."

"Mommy," Leeba wailed, "it could have been me up there with those girls."

"Yes, Mamele, I know." said Leeba's mother. "I thank *Hashem* for that." Leeba told her mother about Ella and why she didn't go on the Ferris wheel.

"Oh, Mamele," cried Leeba's mother, "I'm so proud of you and look how *Hashem* paid you back for being so considerate and kind."

"But, Mommy," said Leeba, "I really didn't want to be with Ella. I really wanted to be on the Ferris wheel."

"I know, dear," said her mother, "but you didn't do what you wanted to do. You did the thing that was right."

The doorbell rang. "I'll get it," said Leeba's mother. Leeba followed her. She opened the door. There stood Ella and her mother.

"We really can't stay but Ella begged me to come to bring her here. She wants to give something to Leeba."

Ella was holding something in her hand. She gave it to Leeba.

It was a little wooden puppy, sad and lovable, almost like the one in the store.

"I . . . h-h-had . . . one . . . j-j-just . . . like . . . it . . . at home . . . It . . . is . . . yours." She smiled her crooked smile. Leeba smiled back.

"Thank you, Ella. It's the nicest present I've ever gotten."

Dov Dov and the Snowbird

The whispering whiteness enfolded Dov Dov in a soft rustling as he walked home from school. He breathed deeply and watched his breath spread on the air before him in white gasps. The air was filled with whirling snow. Drifts gently covered the ground. Icicles glittered under the pale winter sun.

It was hard to see where he was walking. Dov Dov's mind was preoccupied. The new project he was doing for school was so difficult. *Derech Eretz* was the theme and his idea was so good. But he just couldn't get the picture in his mind to be the same picture on the poster. If only . . .

Hey, what was that? Dov Dov jerked to a stop. Something red and blue shone through the snow. Dov Dov bent over the object and his heart seemed to stand still in his ribs.

"A little bird," he whispered. "Where did you come from?" He studied the bird in wonderment. It was beautiful. Was the bird alive? It was so wet, so still and stiff. Dov Dov bent lower and picked up the stiff figure.

"Oh — you poor little bird," he whispered softly. "Did you fall out of your nest? Did you get lost when you were flying?"

Dov Dov felt enormous and strong. He felt a sense of wealth and richness. He trembled to hold such an exquisite thing. He put the bird gently under his warm jacket and started running as quickly as he could in the deep snow.

"Abba! Mommy! Come quick! See what I found!"

Dov Dov and the Snowbird / 61

"Why, Dov Dov," said his mother. "Where did you find the little thing?"

"Is it alive, Mommy, Abba, is it? Is it?"

Dov Dov's father examined the bird. "I think it's breathing. Birds may be motionless and cold, but warmth can sometimes revive them."

They found an old shoe box, lined it with a soft towel and put it near the radiator. They put warm water and bread crumbs near it.

"Will it live, Abba, will it?" asked Dov Dov.

"Maybe," said his father. "The main thing is to keep it warm and well fed. The rest is up to *Hashem*. We'll see."

Dov Dov sat and watched the bird for a long time. "My little snowbird," he whispered.

"In the meantime, young man," said his father, "you'd better get your homework done. There's not much more you can do for the little fellow."

"Oh, Abba, the only homework I have is to finish my *Derech Eretz* project and I already tried making it but I can't."

"Well, try again."

"But I tried two times already."

"So, try three times, four times, five times. Whatever!"

"But I can't do it!"

"How do you know that you can't if you don't keep working at it?"

"What is it you're trying to do?" asked Dov Dov's mother.

"It's a large poster," said Dov Dov. "In the middle I wrote the words *Derech Eretz Kadmah LeTorah*. In the background I drew a *Sefer Torah* and then I drew different examples of *Derech Eretz*. In one box I have a boy getting up to give his seat to an older man on the bus. In another, I have a boy saying "please" to a younger brother. In another box I wrote not to interrupt someone when he's speaking. In another box there is a boy saying "thank you" to his mother for supper."

"It sounds like a very good idea," said his mother.

"But it just doesn't come out right."

"Well, keep on trying, Dov Dov," said his mother. "It certainly won't get done if you stop trying."

"I just don't feel like trying to do it anymore. What's the use of trying if I know it won't come out?"

His father gave Dov Dov a searching look, "Whether it's going to come out right or not is up to *Hashem*. Your job is just to try."

Tweet! — What was that?

Dov Dov and his parents turned to the radiator. The little bird opened its eyes and beak and was pecking greedily at the food. When it was finished, it seemed restless and fluttered madly.

"Abba, something's wrong with its wing," said Dov Dov. "It can't fly."

"Give it time, Dov Dov," said his father. "It needs time to rest and heal."

The next few days were spent between school and tending to the bird. Every day the bird grew stronger, but it still couldn't fly.

"Oh, little snowbird," said Dov Dov. "You don't know if you're going to fly or not, do you? Only *Hashem* knows that, but you're trying. That's all you can do. You know you have to try. The rest is up to *Hashem*. Keep trying, little snowbird. Keep trying."

He watched in amazement as the little bird struggled and fluttered awkwardly. It pecked Dov Dov's finger in a friendly way. Then slowly, it extended both its wings and gently beat them, testing their strength.

Slowly . . . slowly . . . deeper . . . deeper, then faster and faster. Dov Dov watched in breathless amazement at the bird's struggle and effort.

Slowly, it plowed the air with its wings and scooped the air with its feathers. It darted like a wind-blown leaf and flew to the open window.

Dov Dov watched it circle the yard, its colorful tapered wings outlined against the blue sky. It was a moment of splendor. Dov Dov felt as if he himself were flying with the bird into the unlimited sky.

The bird flew higher and higher. Its course widened. It faced the south, dipped its brilliant wings in steady rhythm and was gone.

Dov Dov smiled happily. "Goodbye, little snowbird. You see, your trying paid off."

He closed the window, walked to his desk and took out his *Derech Eretz* poster and paint set.